The Profit Principle

G.R. Massey

DEDICATION

To Lucas & Kimmie

CONTENTS

1

INTRO

It's 10 a.m. on a Monday. You move your beach chair a few feet closer to the warm, azure blue water that comes ashore in waves to hit your feet. The waiter sets down your made-to-order breakfast and asks, "Will there be anything else?" You answer no as you log into your online bank account to see how much money you made overnight. While this sounds like a dream, it is your reality. A reality that began forming the day you purchased *The Profit Principle.*

In this book, I will walk you step-by-step to creating your on-line business. The Profit Principle program is guaranteed to make you large sums of money if followed closely. How much? Any amount you want, anywhere from a supplement to your current income to your primary source of income. The key to this program is creating an automated system that allows you to make money while you sleep. This book is very straightforward. It will describe a series of steps needed to get to the desired outcome. The steps are numerically ordered but don't necessarily need to be followed in that order, but it would make things a lot easier on you if you did them as such.

What I will explain to you is the process of building an online corporation that you will eventually be able to maintain with little or no effort of your own. That does not mean little or no effort in the beginning. Quite the contrary, a lot will be on your shoulders in the beginning. You must stay focused on each task and pursue them to completion. I know from experience, especially in the case of having a full-time job and a family, it is very easy to get off track. You can lose months if you get tied up in distractions. As I mention many times on my website, this is no 'Get Rich Quick' scam, there's no such thing, and only suckers believe there is. This will work the same as anything in life; you will get out of it what you put into it. However, the goal is that within a year you will have a fully functioning business that does not need you involved in it in order to make a profit, and a huge profit at that.

So now that we have set the stage, let's begin…

2

PHASE ONE: DUE DILLIGENCE

1. Set Up LLC

A Limited Liability Company, or LLC, is a flexible form of
enterprise that blends elements of partnership and corporate
structures. It is a legal form of company that provides limited
liability to its owners in the vast majority of United States
jurisdictions. LLCs do not need to be organized for profit.
You must have your LLC in order to file for a tax ID
number. A tax ID number is like the social security number
for your business. Without a tax ID, you cannot buy
products from manufactures or suppliers or even set up a
company bank account. Your LLC and tax ID number also
allow you to write off your expenses (and you will have a lot)
for tax savings. Many unscrupulous people create an LLC
without even intending to run an actual business, just to
benefit from the tax savings, but unlike those bums you will
be making money! Use freelegalagent.com to find a filing
agent for your LLC. They will allow you to use one of their
agents free for one year. Many other sites will charge you up
to $100 for a filing agent. Don't worry about what a filing

agent does, just know you'll need one and freelegalagent.com will do it free for the first year. Total cost, approximately $200 to complete the LLC process, check with your Secretary of State office to file online.

2. Buy copy of Quicken or QuickBooks

All real businesses have to keep an eye on their finances. Without the accounting side taken care of, all you really have is a hobby. In the very beginning if money is a concern, you may want to use Excel to track your finances, but eventually you want to upgrade to Quicken or QuickBooks. These allow you to track inventory, P&L (profit & loss), and expenses, along with many other needed tools. They even let you print a nice financial statement at the end of the year for tax purposes. They pull this information automatically from your business bank account or credit card, making life a lot easier. Let me tell you from experience, if you do not take care of this vital aspect of your business you will have no real idea of how much money you're making or losing. Some flashy products you may want to sell, when examined through the financial prism, won't look so flashy. You may not be making what you think, and you could be losing money on each item you sell! QuickBooks now has an online option in which you pay a monthly fee instead of a onetime fee; I suggest using the online option if money is an issue since it is a lot cheaper up front.

3. Set Up Bank Account in Company Name

This is easy, yet a lot of people new in business don't do it. You have your LLC & tax ID. Meet with someone at your local bank to open a business account, along with a debit or credit card (if you're approved). Once you set up your bank account ONLY buy items used for the business out of this account. There are a lot of expenses you'll use this account for, but be careful not to use this account for the family trip to Disney, or else you risk the dreaded audit come tax time.

Inventory, shipping, packaging, advertising, company-related travel, company related meals, equipment, computers, etc., and company-related uniforms are all examples of items traditionally purchased from the company account.

4. **Create Company Email Address**

In business, it is very important to have a consistent brand. On the Internet, it all begins with your email address. There are various services out there that let you use your own name for the domain. Go Daddy and Domain.com are two of the most popular. I suggest this route with an info@businessname.com and then rerouting that email address to Gmail. Gmail has the best mail-searching mechanisms of any other email host, and you will need to be able to search your email often. It also has a lot of other cool features in the Gmail Labs sections that are useful, such as canned responses, labels, and Signatures. Oh yeah, and it's free to use.

5. **Order Free Boxes from the Post Office - All Sizes and Shapes and don't forget Packaging Sleeves**

The beginning of *The Profit Principle* system calls for you to do all of the shipping yourself. When shipping, you will need certain packing supplies, boxes being the most important. The United States Postal Service gives away a number of boxes for free, and you will do a large percentage of your shipping via USPS.com because of the lower cost compared to FedEx & UPS. Google the phrase "USPS Free Supplies" and you will get a link to the Postal Services' website where you can order free priority boxes as well as flat-rate boxes. Priority boxes are good for products of a variety of dimensions and weights. However, flat rate boxes are good for small, heavy items. Flat rate boxes costs are flat to ship items below 70 lbs. This is recommended for heavier items because in shipping lighter items, the flat rate price is higher than priority.

The United States Postal Service website offers free packaging slips as well. It's a lot easier to attach your label using these packaging slips than trying to tape them to each box. One thing to keep in mind is that you can only use these free boxes with the post office. UPS, DHL & FedEx do not accept these boxes. If you attempt you use these boxes with a different carrier, the carrier will reject them from being sent. To order the boxes, go to the USPS website and follow the free supply links. Make sure you order a mixed lot of box sizes.

6. **Setup Uline, Office Depot, etc. Accounts**

As you start to sell larger sized items or items being shipped via FedEx, UPS, or DHL, you will need more supplies than the Postal Service Office can offer for free. Companies like Uline & Office Depot offer a full range of items you will need to ship your items. They also have a large range of box sizes. This is a must. These companies usually have a local pickup warehouse and the option to ship to your home. Below is a short list of basic items you should have on hand before you begin shipping your products.

Necessary Shipping Supplies

- Boxes of various dimensions(from USPS and Uline)

- Shipping scale

- Packing Tape

- Bubble Wrap

- Kraft paper (to stuff the boxes)

7. Set Up P.O. Box

Post Office boxes (P.O. boxes) offer privacy for your business. While you may want your inventory shipped to your home for convenience, you do not want to use your home address for your business address simply because in this day in age some scorned customer may look you up one day and pay a visit. P.O. boxes offer you the privacy to receive all of your mailings without giving up your actual address. Also, when you get to the point of creating your website and promotional emails, you are required by law to include an address and a P.O. box is perfect in this case as well. They are not very expensive, check your local post office or a UPS or Fed Ex store for details.

8. Buy Shipping Scale

Buying a shipping scale is crucial to saving money on outgoing shipments to customers. As you ship items, you have to report the weight each package to the shipping carrier. Don't try to eyeball it. If the weight you estimate is too low (and the carrier WILL re-weigh your package) they'll either return the package to you, increasing the shipping time to your customer, or they will charge you double the difference. If the weight you estimate is too high, you are throwing money away since you are charged based on the packages weight.

A good shipping scale will pay for itself in two weeks. Also, when owning your own scale you can preprint your labels online and avoid standing in line to drop off boxes. An added bonus is that through the U.S. Postal Service, you can schedule at home pickup of packages. Check the USPS.com for further details.

9. **Inkjet Printer**

You will need to print shipping labels. Again, you DO NOT want to stand in line at a shipping center with an armful of boxes. It is very time consuming and a pain. Note: Be sure while you are buying these items you are entering these expenses into Quicken or QuickBooks, as these are tax deductable.

10. **Computer**

Although it might seem a given, get something reliable; it doesn't need to be a super computer but something that can handle the web and apps fairly quickly. If you're able to operate the MS Office suite without a hitch and can check your Facebook account with no problem, then that computer will likely be fine. I prefer a laptop so that I am mobile, but the choice is completely up to you.

11. **Google Voice**

Google Voice is a free service that allows you to own and operate a separate number. With this number, you can setup custom voice mails, store voice mails online, and a host of other features. You will be asked by eBay, Amazon, etc. to give a number where they may reach you and this is the number you should use. You want to keep as much of your business separate from your personal life as possible, and the ability to create a separate voicemail is really neat, especially when customers need to contact you.

12. Reliable Internet Service

If you have dial up, it's time to upgrade. There are too many internet transactions that will take place for you to waste time with the whistle and fax screech. Any package using cable or DSL will work.

13. Designate an Area in Home for Inventory

This is often an overlooked step but it is needed and will benefit you to have this area prepared *before* your products arrive. Use a spare room, garage, or closet; any place in your home you can put things and have them out of the way without disturbing the rest of the household. This applies to those who live alone as well. If you fail to do this, your inventory will take over your house: the kitchen, bathroom, even on top of the TV. The next thing you know, product will get lost or damaged. Find some room for your inventory on the front end and you'll be much happier as you ramp up.

14. Designate an Area in Home to Work on Business

This may or may not be in the same room you store your inventory. I recommend if you're using a room for your inventory, try to set up your workspace in that room as well. If it's in a garage, then try and use an adjacent room. This will be your area for packaging and labeling shipments, and making correspondences using the computer. This area IS your company and it needs to be one designated area. As you grow, you'll setup processes in your area that make the jobs a lot easier. My stapler is right here, my tape gun there, etc. It will become second nature after a while because this is where you are each and *every time* you work. You may move your laptop to other rooms when needed, but your packing and shipping center needs to be the same area.

15. Smartphone

This would include any mobile phone where you can receive and respond to emails: Blackberry, iPhone, etc. They are very easy to set up with your email account, and now you have 24/7 access to customer inquiries. Eventually you won't need this, but during this beginning stage you want always to be able to answer simple customer questions right away. More complicated questions can wait until you are near your work computer, but I have found that interested customers will be more likely to purchase from you when you respond to them quickly. Sometimes they may just want to know if you ship to their country, or if you'll accept a few dollars less than your listed price. Those sorts of questions can be answered quickly from your Smartphone wherever you are.

16. Create Logo

Now that you have a company name, a good professional logo is needed. You will use this logo throughout eBay or Amazon as well as on your thank-you letters to customers that go out with each shipment. Unless you have experience, do not attempt to create a logo on your own. There are many places online where you can get a professional team of artists to create you a logo for $25 to $100. I suggest taking this route and getting a logo that you can be proud of. Google the term, "Custom Logo Design" to get started.

17. Create Company Account with UPS, Fed Ex

Some heavier items are cheaper to ship domestically using UPS and FedEx. Go to their websites and create a business account. I find UPS to be cheaper than FedEx, but it depends on what you sell, where you live, and where you are shipping your product. You will have to use the shipping calculators on each site to find out exact prices and compare. Eventually, you'll just know what an item costs to ship just about anywhere whenever you use USPS, FedEx, or UPS. Also, when you receive items from your supplier or shipping supplies, you should use your UPS or FedEx account numbers. The cost will be billed to your corporate bank account later, and it will build a shipping history that will eventually get you discounts when using your account number.

18. Experian or Dun & Bradstreet: Create Company Credit Profile

In the beginning you may need to use your personal credit card or cash to buy the things you need for your business, but eventually you will want to obtain lines of credit using your businesses purchase and repayment history. Experian and Dun &Bradstreet are where you begin this process. Once you set up your company account, all of the transactions made using your company credit/debit cards are recorded as they would with paying a bill on time with your personal credit. Eventually you will be able to obtain business credit cards, and the ability to go to the bank and obtain lines of credit. This will not be something you can do overnight, but the more business you do, the shorter until that time comes. You'll need your tax ID and bank account info to register; cost is $100 to $150.

19. Business Cards

You may ask, "If I'm running an online business do I REALLY need business cards?" The answer is, "Why not?" Quality business cards are so cheap to create nowadays it doesn't make sense not to have business cards. There are sites online where you can get 50 business cards created and shipped to you for seven or eight bucks. You never know whom you may bump into throughout your day, and a quality business card speaks volumes when presenting someone with your business. Secret: One trick to being taken seriously with your business card is not to put on your title CEO, President, Owner, Founder or anything like that. People can usually tell how big your business is when speaking with you briefly, so in the beginning just put your name and contact info. It doesn't make you seem self-absorbed and still accomplishes the task. Whenever I speak to a new entrepreneur and see CEO or something boisterous, I assume it's a one-man shop and most likely struggling, if doing any business at all.

20. Set Up eBay, Amazon, Craigslist account with Company Name or Similar

If you haven't already set up your account on eBay and Amazon, use your company name and logo where applicable. On eBay, sign up for selling manager pro, it will make listing and relisting products a lot easier. Amazon is easy to set up, look for "Your Account," from there just fill in your account info, remember to use your P.O. Box address and your Google Voice number. Amazon requires you to enter some personal information as well. That's no problem; the customer will never know it's coming from you.

21. **Set Up PayPal and Google Checkout Account with Company Name and Tax ID.**

eBay does not have payment a mechanism within its site so you need to sign up with PayPal. For the sake of selling on eBay, you can set up your PayPal account as personal, then go into your profile, and change it to a business account. Be sure to have your tax identification and banking info ready.

3

PHASE TWO: THE BASICS

eBay – Existing products

All right, now that we gotten our due diligence done we can begin on how to actually MAKE money ;-). Follow the steps below and my program will work for you as it is working for me. The next section will walk you through getting your existing products listed on eBay and Amazon. Even if you don't have anything ready, please find SOMETHING, even if you have to go to a garage sale just to find a knick-knack to sell. You ABSOLUTELY have to sell something initially in order to get started properly.

1. **Inventory Your Products**

   All right, so your mom has found your old baseball card collection, or you want to sell your old Barbie's, the process will be the same for successful listings. Some of this part may be found in other, "How to Sell on eBay" type of books, which is fine. This part is essential, and the building blocks to implementing The Profit PrincipleThe Profit Principle system, and I have a unique take on these principles that will not be found any other book of this type, so pay attention!

The first thing you need to do in MS Excel or Word is write down the name and brand of your existing products and include any detail. For example, you have a Don Mattingly baseball card, the details would be "Second-year Yankees Don Mattingly from Topps in Mint Condition, 1984." Those are the pertinent details that eBay users may use to search for this card. Even though these are the pertinent details, if you were to enter this into a search you would most likely come back with few or no results. You have to try to find a more concise way of entering this information. Let's try "Topps Don Mattingly 1984'. Bingo! Now we'll get results. Click on the auction of one of the listings that show up to see details, you may see "Yankee's' and "Mint condition' listed as well. Take a look at the card being listed. Does it look like the card you have? If yes, then enter this card on your spreadsheet using the search term you had success with: "Topps Don Mattingly 1984'. This is your first product. Go through and perform this process on all of the items you're planning to sell.

a. Write out as much product detail as possible.
b. Try a search using those details.
c. Use more concise terms.
d. Once you generate results, click details to make sure your details match those of the identical items being sold currently on eBay.
e. Verify that the pictures are the same.
f. Enter product into spreadsheet using search term that displayed results.

2. Price-compare Your Items

Now that you have identified and recorded all of the items you plan to sell on your spreadsheet, it's time to see what those items are selling for in eBay so that we may price our items appropriately. Most eBay books tell you to search for your product and base your price on what they are selling for. This is an immature approach, since anyone can list a product at any price, it doesn't mean it ever sold. So using this approach, you could, and probably would be wasting your money from the listing itself. What we will do is search the SOLD listings. What was the price, description photo, etc. that actually made a sale, thus increasing our sold-to-listed ratio and saving money. First, let's go back to our selling spreadsheet; let's start with our first entry, "Topps Don Mattingly 1984." In eBay, just to the right of the "Search" button you'll see a link to the "Advanced Options," click "Advanced Options."

a. Enter keyword or item number: Topps Don Mattingly 1984
b. Search Include, Completed listing Check
c. Auction format, Buy it now: Check, Check
d. Search

You'll see in red letters, listings that failed to sell and at what price they failed to do so. You'll also see in green, those listings that were successful. This is a crucial lesson to learn. Pay close attention to the things on the listings that failed.

i. One, check the photo of the item, is it a stock photo or an actual photo taken by the seller?
ii. Is the description any good?

iii. What was the price listed? How did that price compare to what others were selling for?

iv. How much feedback does this person selling this item have? Is the feedback good?

v. How much were they charging for shipping?

vi. What time did this auction end, and was that at a time when people are typically online buying products?

All of these factors need to be taken into consideration. Let's look at each in detail.

a. Photo – Whether you're selling an item you already have in your possession or if you're using a stock photo found online, it needs to look good. Many times when sellers are selling an item said to be in their possession, buyers want to see that actual item; they don't want a stock photo of the 1984 Don Mattingly Baseball card, they know what is should look like. They want to see an actual photo of the item you are selling. Invest in a decent digital camera (buy with company account, add to QuickBooks), nowadays even most Smartphone's will take good enough pictures for you to post a quality shot. Don't rush, take a few shots from different angles, depending on the item you're selling close-up shots may help as well

b. Description – This is usually pretty easy, if you know what you're selling you can usually just find a website that describes the product best and copy their text. Be sure to double check the description to make sure it's not promising a free back massage with every purchase. Also you'll want to add, maybe at the top, a "International Shipping Available", "Mint Condition", for used items those two in bold at the top reduce questions that people may ask.

c. Price – Don't price the item too high or too low. When compared to others selling the same or similar items, are you too high? Maybe too low, sometimes buyers are wary of items they know to be worth $100 selling for $20. It screams scam to them. You have to be in that "sweet spot" when it comes to price, and this means checking your competition prior to pricing your item.

d. Feedback – Ahh, feedback, the single most important factor to your success on eBay. Screw this up and you may as well kill the eBay store and create a new one. No matter how awesome your wares, nobody will purchase anything from you if you have 40 percent positive feedback! If you have too little feedback while trying to sell a medium to high priced item and you may suffer as well. Yes, when examining the failed listings, click the user's feedback rating and read the recent comments and look at the percentage. Every seller gets bad feedback every now and then, but for the most part you need to keep your feedback over 98 percent to have a chance of being successful using *The Profit Principle* program in order to make REAL money, and especially in the beginning. Get ten positive feedbacks and two negatives, guess what your rating will be?...Not good enough.

e. Shipping fees – In the beginning, you can judge what you should charge for shipping by looking at the competition. Stay in this range and you will be OK. For international shipping, use the calculated shipping option and charge $3 or so for S&H and you will be in a good range to make a sale. Shipping prices are very important, and sometimes you'll see that you can take $5 off the item price and add that to the shipping price, and a lot of people will buy from you not taking the time to add the two up ☺

f. What time did the auction end? You'll find that most of the action online is between the hours of 7 p.m. and 11 p.m. PST. Sunday, Monday, and Tuesday, in that order. Sunday and Monday at those times are the hottest. With this in mind, and the way eBay moves the listing nearing completion to the top of the others when searched, we want our listing to end in these time slots on these days. The most popular eBay listings are the auctions. The auctions allow you to start the bidding at a certain price and people can bid up the price. The other popular format Is Buy it Now or BIN. This works similar to other ecommerce sites in that you have a fixed price for the item and you input what you're willing to sell it for and the amount of inventory you carry. Both of these options run for various amounts of days, the recommended amount being seven. Until you get your feedback up, eBay does not allow you to schedule your listing for a future date and time, you'll have to create them and they will begin immediately. With this in mind, and the fact that we want them to end on certain days at certain times (KEEP IN MIND EBAY OPERATES ON PACIFIC TIME), we want to create our listings to begin at 7:30 p.m. PST This covers the hot period throughout the entire country and our listings will end during this period when most buy. This will increase the probability of your item selling, guaranteed.

3. Undersell Your Competition

Once you've run this search you see in green the prices that sold. Now try listing your item for a little less than the selling price of the items that won. Since you are new, you have to have some compelling strategy to sell your items. You will be faced with competition that has been doing business for years, and they will have good feedback to prove it. Study those businesses that have the great feedback and learn from them, but don't dare be intimidated by them. At the end of the day people want what they want at the lowest price possible, and you will find people who are willing to take a chance on you if the price is right.

4. Method to List Your Products

I'm not going to go into too much detail about "How to list on eBay". It's pretty straightforward and eBay provides plenty of tutorials to help you. There are, however, a few tricks that I like to use when listing.

a. ALWAYS USE CAPS FOR TITLE. Capitalize your title and that will set it apart from your competition. eBay tries to charge you for every little perk in a listing, but to simply use capitalization in your title is usually enough to get attention.

b. Take good pics if you have the item on hand, use high-resolution stock photos for items you don't have on hand. Don't be lazy with the pictures unless you don't want your item to sell.

c. In the description always display in caps the following text prior to describing the item: "BRAND NEW IN STOCK (or whatever the item's condition), INTERNATIONAL SHIPPING AVAILABLE". I know this seems simple but you'd be surprised by how many people ask these questions if you don't include them in big bold letters.

d. For the item description, just steal someone else's from the web. Don't try to describe the item yourself. Just skim it to make sure you take out any company-specific verbiage or promises. Once you find a good company that has great descriptions, keep using them.

e.   Use the hidden counter on items.

f.   Make sure that you are listing on Sunday, Monday or Tuesday nights, using seven-day auction or fixed price.

g.   You may lose a little money in the beginning to get customers, auction a listing or two at around your cost or a little less than you'd accept on the item. It may not get to the price you eventually want, but you'll be close and gain a customer and eventually feedback, which is crucial.

h.   If you do a fixed-price item, never list that you have more than three items available. If you enter 11 eBay will show that you have 11 as "more than 10". Customers don't tend to buy if they think you have plenty remaining in stock, and will come back later or price shop. If you list that you have two it creates a since of urgency, which is what you want. "Buy this item now because you may come back later and it is no longer available," is what you want them thinking.

i.   Use flat pricing, shipping domestically. Check your competition prices and price yours slightly lower. For international shipping, use calculated based on the weight. Use USPS priority. Add $3 for shipping and handling.

j.   Handling time set to one day, nobody really holds you to that and it looks good in the listing.

5.   Ship with Good Business Practices.

In the next phase we will talk about fulfillment centers and how they ship out your products for you, but during this phase YOU need to ship out all of your products yourself. You will receive an email from eBay letting you know if your product sold or not. If it didn't sell, be sure to relist it. You may have to lower the price a little or tweak a few things here and there in order for it to sell again. Maybe you need to experiment with the time the auction ends.

If your item has sold, now is when you need to have everything in order in your "working" room. If you have time, the night it sells go ahead and put your item into a box, add any necessary protection and ship it through PayPal. When you log into PayPal, you will see the items you sold along with an option to ship. Ship using whatever method was agreed upon in eBay. You will usually make a few bucks in shipping, so if you aren't you need to re-evaluate what you're charging the customers. I've found UPS to be cheaper for domestic shipping for heavier boxes, and you are able to select the UPS option in PayPal.

Before you seal you box be sure to include a "Thank You" letter. This letter will include a simple message thanking the customer for their purchase; include your logo, address, and maybe a signature. Also, *and this is huge*, be sure to add a line asking the customer to leave you GREAT feedback on this transaction through eBay. Many people forget to leave feedback, but this will increase the percentages in your favor. A kind, direct "Thank You" letter is intended to bring customers back and remind them to leave feedback.

Once you've packaged your item and printed your label, use the see-through label jacket you received from the USPS for free to house the label and affix it to your box. Now, if you're lazy like me and don't feel like taking my boxes to the post office all you have to do is schedule a pickup with the USPS and they will pick your boxes up from your home FOR FREE (http://www.usps.com/pickup/welcome.htm). UPS and Fed Ex also have a pickup service but it's not free. They charge you based on the total weight of you boxes, it's not very expensive but if you're selling items with a very small margin it may be better to find a UPS or Fed Ex store to drop them off. Once you're selling a lot, it makes more sense to have a pickup with USPS and UPS/FedEx regardless of the costs.

6. Feedback harassment.

I hate to use the word harassment, but that's really what it is. In eBay if you look through your sold items you will see stars by those who have left you positive feedback, you need to "remind" those who haven't to leave feedback. As we progress through this program, you will rely more and more on great feedback so you cannot allow great transactions to go unnoticed and undocumented. There is an option in eBay to send email to customer, use that to remind them about it. Most people just forget, so be tactful in your email.

7. Track your finances with Excel and QuickBooks.

Since everything you're selling is already in your possession and paid for it will be all profit and an easy accounting job. If you don't pay attention to your money, you absolutely are not running a BUSINESS. You have a HOBBY. A business' only purpose is to make money; to do this you must have a good grasp on your numbers. How much did that item really cost me? In the case of someone who already had the item in their possession this will be different and a lot simpler. You still have items to take into consideration though. Costs to ship will include the box and shipping material if you purchased these separately. What about the shipping paper, did you already own a printer, computer, tape gun? These are items you may have already inputted into QB as office supplies. eBay is going to charge you around 9 percent per transaction and PayPal is close to four percent, so those also need to be taken into consideration. Whether you're using Excel, Quickbooks, or whatever, you need to figure out after your item sells how much profit per item did you really make, and adding up the profit if it covers any equipment you had to purchase. I prefer Quickbooks because eBay allows you to import your sales data directly into your QuickBooks company profile. If you don't take my advice in any other parts of this book take this, ALWAYS PAY ATTENTION to your accounting information.

eBay – No Existing Products, Beginner

There have been many people since eBay's inception that have quit their jobs and made hundreds of thousands, and even millions of dollars, selling products they purchased wholesale elsewhere. It always sounds so easy, "we found this great product and things just took off from there." The reality is that it really can be easy if you know what you're doing. I spent countless hours and money in the beginning trying to figure out what to sell and where to get it. Below are many techniques I've developed over the years that are guaranteed to be successful if followed properly.

1. **Choosing the Best Products to Sell**

So you may think you're going to go out and sell a bunch of iPods or iPhones, or maybe video games and music. The reality is you're not, and if you do you're not going to make ANY money, in fact you'll lose thousands. You know why? It's because everybody and their momma is selling the popular stuff on eBay and elsewhere. You have no chance, trust me; don't waste your time. Here is a good rule of thumb when looking for items to buy. "If the customer is able to get into their car and drive to a store to purchase this product, stay away." That means anything usually sold at a Wal-Mart, BestBuy, Toys R Us, and any major chain retail store, period. STAY AWAY! Nine times out of 10, even if you are able to find a place to source the products usually sold in these stores you would not make any money. You cannot compete with a BestBuy on the price of a new iPad, Best Buy buys iPads by the millions, so who do you think Apple is going to give their best price to; you or BestBuy? Sorry if I'm beating this into the ground but this is something worth beating. I can't count how many people I've mentored who swear that they are going to make their first million selling GPS systems and going head to head with the big boys.

What we're after is a niche, actually a niche within a niche. Toys are a category, a niche would be Sci-Fi memorabilia and niche within a niche would be Star Trek collectible action figures. You're not going to go into a Toys R Us and find a recreated eight-inch Spock character from the second Star Trek movie. This is the ideal product, something your customer has to come to you for, a niche within a niche. Common niches are antiques, sport and music memorabilia, collectible items, specialized sporting gear, etc.

This is the most time-consuming portion of *The Profit Principle* program, but it will be the cornerstone of everything to come, so it will pay for you to take your time here in selecting your product.

Another important rule is to "Sell What Sells". Meaning, even if you don't have an interest in 19th century British medallions, if you are able to source them and find a customer base that allows you to make a profit, you need to sell this item. Remember it's about MAKING MONEY. Even you don't know a lot about that topic, you will learn enough in time. With tools like Google, Twitter, &

Facebook, you can find out just about anything known to man.

These series of steps below will help you in narrowing down to the product you should sell. Considering that antiques, sports, and music memorabilia, collectibles items, specialized sporting gear are the most common areas in eBay you'll be able to find a niche within each. Start with Music memorabilia.

How to Find: "Sell What Sells"

a. Type, 'Music memorabilia' in eBay – search and see what comes back.
b. You'll see antique instruments, clothing, autographs, gold records, and a bunch or other subcategories.
c. These are all just examples of music memorabilia, now search for "Pink Floyd gold records."
d. What we did was choose a niche (music memorabilia) and take a niche within that niche (Pink Floyd or Rock & Roll). We paired Pink Floyd with one of the listing titles that came up when we searched for music memorabilia.
e. You should see a lot of listings for Pink Floyd gold records that are currently selling. Let's see if they're actually being SOLD and at what price.
f. Remember to do an "Advanced' search on completed items and search for "Pink Floyd gold record."
g. BINGO! You should see some items sold. (If you don't, choose another artist and run a similar search, i.e. Elvis, Rolling Stones, The Beatles etc.) Click one of the listings that won and let's see the details. Pay attention to how it was presented description-wise, as well as its price and the seller's feedback

8. What Sells Regularly?

What you really want is a product or niche that has consistent sales over a time period. Run the "Sell What Sells" searches over and over on different NWN's (Niche within Niches) and you'll see that some have more sales than others. Those are the products we need to source IF AND ONLY IF we find suppliers that sell them and sell them at a price where we can make a profit!

9. Locating a Supplier

What is a supplier? Let's start with the manufacturer. The manufacturer designs and creates the widget, they may have a factory in Asia but all rights to that widget are theirs. The manufacturer produces one million widgets a year, many of which are shipped out to retail stores all over the world. The widgets are also purchased by suppliers by the thousands; in fact the only way the supplier can buy directly from the manufacturer is if they buy at least 1,000 widgets and if they want more they have to continue to purchase in increments of 1,000. Then there is you, the online retailer. For all intents and purposes, you are a "Mom & Pop" store. You want to sell these widgets but you can't afford to purchase 1,000 at a time. If only there were a way you could buy the widgets at maybe a quantity of 10 or 20. That, my friends, is where the supplier comes in, you will purchase most of your inventory from the supplier, of course you may pay a lot more than the supplier has but remember the supplier purchased 1,000 widgets and has taken a huge risk in doing so. You may over time develop relationships with manufactures and count your blessings if you are ever able to do so. However, in the beginning to ramping up phases of your business, a few good suppliers are worth their weight in gold.

10. Fake Suppliers? BEWARE!

So now you know what a supplier is, how do you go about finding a reputable supplier for the product you'd like to sell? Well I will give you a tip, World Wide Brands. Again, here is another aspect of this business I did not understand in the beginning; I thought that I could just Google: "Pink Floyd Gold Records wholesale" for example, and whatever popped up would be where I should buy my inventory. The reality is much worse; there are actually middlemen between the manufacturer and supplier and middlemen between the supplier and you. All of them taking a cut and driving the price up. I recommend using Worldwide Brands to find your suppliers because they do background checks on all of the so-called suppliers. It's not cheap, but once you're in you're in for life, no monthly fees. You can search for all kinds of products using their database. In reference to our Pink Floyd music memorabilia, you can do a search for "music memorabilia' in Worldwide Brands and you will see a list of available suppliers. If you click on one of the suppliers, you will be given an option to submit an application. I recommend looking through their website to make sure their products are within the same category you're looking for. While you're at it, look up some of their other products in eBay to see what they're selling for. If you see your target product along many of their other products selling well on eBay, then go ahead and submit an application with them, you will need your tax ID number in order to do so.

SalesHoo is another site similar to Worldwide Brands; they vet each supplier to make sure they are directly in touch with the manufacturer and not middlemen of middlemen. I believe they are a little cheaper than Worldwide Brands but do not have the same amount of suppliers available.

11. Doing Business with a Supplier

Now that you have identified a supplier or two, let's move ahead and make an order. Identify the product(s) you would like to try to sell. There are a few things that need to be considered PRIOR to ordering from the supplier:

a. How many items does the supplier require? Some suppliers let you purchase at a wholesale one unit, some up to 40. It really depends, if you know you want to sell a widget, but the supplier requires you to buy 25 widgets to get the discount, then you have to ask yourself, "How fast do I think I can sell these?" If you don't think you can move 25 units in a month, I would not recommend you not purchasing that item. You must consider your competition; let's say you order 25 and you sell 10 in the first week. You're feeling great, but then you notice you're halfway into week two and you've only sold one, you know why? It's likely because you're competition has increased. Other sellers have received their stock of this item or they saw you selling a bunch and decided to drop their price under yours to steal your business. So now a widget that was selling for $10 a pop in week one is now only worth $9, and let's say you purchased each widget for $5. That still leaves a $4 profit, but remember that price will continue to drop until everyone runs out of stock. It will get to the point where you are losing money each time you sell an item. If you can't move them quick, don't purchase large quantities. Use the JIT inventory approach. JIT stands for Just in Time, you only want to keep just enough inventory to appease demand, anything else will result in a loss of your money.

b. "What is the real cost?" Let's say again that the widget's price is $5 per wholesale and let's say you only order 10. You must factor into this price 12 percent for the shipping fees from the supplier to you. So ($50 x .12) +50 = $56.

We must also factor into this price the cost of outgoing boxes and shipping supplies per item. Let's say it will be $1.50 per outgoing item. So $56 + $11.50 (10 boxes) = $67.50/10 = $6.75/widget

Now we must consider what we plan to sell these units for in eBay. We want to try to sell these $5 widgets for at least $10 on eBay. eBay will take around 9 percent commission and PayPal is going to take around 3.5 percent. So let's take $10 x .125 = $1.25. Finally, we take $6.75 (REAL widget price) +$1.25 (eBay and PayPal commission) = $8. So $8 is the REAL price per item, which means that if we are able to consistently sell each widget for at least $10 we are making about a 20 percent profit, which is fantastic!

You can apply this formula to any item you are planning to purchase. You can create a macro in QuickBooks to do this automatically, or a formula in Excel. This is a VITAL part of selecting which items to sell. Always give yourself wiggle room in the margin for price flux and competition. Many times that price you have in mind to sell the item at will have to be lowered in order to continue to attract customers. Using the example above, we're at a 20 percent margin, most likely the last few units of that widget may get down to a 5 percent or even a slight net loss. This is because of the competition; you just want to get in and get out as fast as possible and move on to a different item to sell.

This all really gets fun when you start dealing with the high-priced items. You can really make some great money fast. Just remember to do your homework and order tentatively.

12. Do a Test Order

Now that you have several products within the NWN and you have vetted them through our "what is the real cost" analysis, now it's time to get in the game. Using your COMPANY debit or credit card, you can now make an order through your supplier of choice. Start with a small order, very small and let's see how this process works with them. Some suppliers ship out your products faster than others. The customer support varies as well, as does the packaging they use when shipping your items. Give the supplier of choice your FedEx or UPS account number to use when shipping your items. You want to begin building a history with them as well. This history will lead to discounts down the road. You're ready. Make your first order!

Once you receive confirmation from your supplier that the package is being shipped, you can now post that product on eBay. Even if your product sells before the seven days that the listing runs, and even if your product hasn't arrived yet you are fine. Just make sure when it does arrive you ship the product out in the order each order was received.

13. Sell & Ship!

Make sure all of you packaging is neat, your letter is written well with no grammar issues or typos. Also remember to schedule a pickup either with USPS or UPS when you're done, this will make your life a lot easier, I promise.

14. Track in Your Finances

As I've mentioned nearly 700 times at this point, track everything in QuickBooks, QuickBooks has an option to add inventory. This is especially needed for this module of selling, where you're buying and selling products all the time.

15. Increase Product Supply

In the beginning if you are selling 5 to 10 different products, you're good. Any more than that will get confusing. As you become more and more used to selling, you can increase your numbers. You also need to find more than one supplier. Most products are sold through multiple suppliers, so sign up to at least two; this gives you more options when it comes to ordering from a price standpoint and provides you with an additional source for product. You don't want to spend hours on eBay figuring out what to sell, only for it to sell out at the supplier when you're ready to buy!

4

PHASE THREE: THE SECRET SAUCE

This section will teach you about pre-orders, or pre-sales, as some refer to it. This section is the reason you bought this system, this is the behind-the-scenes look at how David Copperfield made the Statue of Liberty disappear. This is the truth about Area 59. This is where, if done properly, you can get RICH. Some of the things I discuss below may seem risqué, just know that they are 100 percent legal and are allowed in eBay although not advertised. This is where I made most of my mistakes initially and eventually made most of my money. If you follow my instructions below you will avoid making thousands of dollars of mistakes and will set yourself up to make HUGE amount of cash!

Pre-Orders

1. Pre-Order Explanation

A pre-order is an order placed for an item that has not yet been released. The concept for pre-orders came about when people found it hard to get popular items in stores once they were released unless they were first in line. Companies were then given the idea to allow people to reserve their own personal copy, before the release, which has been a huge success. Pre-orders allow consumers to guarantee prompt delivery on release, manufacturers can gauge how much demand there will be, and hence how large initial production runs should be, and sellers can be assured of minimum sales. Additionally, high pre-order rates can be used to generate publicity to further increase sales.

Large retailers have been using pre-orders for a very long time. However, its usage in online retail is just now picking up and its practice is still only used by the big boys, leaving a huge opportunity for small to medium retailers to generate a large amount of revenue quickly, as long as they are able to deliver on their promise. What I have learned is that your success in selling via pre-order is about the customer's trust.

2. Pre-order Execution

The Pre-order section is in the middle of *The Profit Principle* program on purpose. It is the heart of my system and the largest reason for its success, but I feel that in order to understand the power of the pre-order you should start selling "in-stock" items and selling them for a while. This will allow you to learn how to sell online and run your business before getting involved in pre-orders. Pre-order management can be complicated, so if you do not have a firm grasp of selling in-stock items you will likely fail. Also, since pre-order success is largely dependent on customer trust, it is better to build your feedback up to at least 15 positives in eBay before attempting a pre-order. What we will be doing is selling and receiving payment for an item that we do not have in our possession. Most online retailers do not require payment until the product is in stock, but eBay does. So this is where it can be tricky. Some of your more savvy customers will ask why they are being required to pay upfront for the item, but most won't notice. For those savvy customers, you can just say that eBay requires upfront payment on all transactions. Many times if they cannot find that product being pre-sold online, they will end up ordering from you. I'd say 98 percent don't even ask that, but I'd also say about 50 percent don't pay attention that it is a pre-order, so if they haven't received their product in a week they will be sending you crazy emails. Also, in eBay you have up until 30 days from the time your item was ordered for it to be delivered, so again we have to be careful but I will teach you how to deal with this rule and your customers. It's all about communication. If you overly communicate the status to your customers in a personable manner, they will wait forever.

3. Finding Sellable Pre-orders

The first step in selling pre-orders is identifying a niche that is constantly updating and pre-selling its products. Sci-fi collectables, music & TV memorabilia, sports memorabilia, and coins are a few of my favorites. Stay away from electronics, clothing, antiques, etc. Anything that either you cannot buy at a good price or things that do not typically have pre-orders to sell. In my recommended products, you will find an endless supply of products with newer products being sold through the suppliers you find on Worldwide Brands or Saleshoo. In Sci-fi for example, you'll find endless Star Track busts coming out for all of their characters. Imagine the breath of content manufacturers have to pull from when considering what new product they'd like to build. They list their pre-orders and wait and see customer demand, once they've gauged a successful product, they start production. What products do I sell? This is always the most common question, Sci-fi collectables, music & TV memorabilia, sports memorabilia, coins. Choose one or two of these to focus on and you will be fine. You'll find success when you drill down to a niche within these niches. Say if you only wanted to focus on rock & rock music memorabilia instead of any genre of music, you could sell any of these actually. It may take you a lot longer to keep up with your accounting records and product listings, but the customer just wants to buy from a reputable company at a decent price. You don't really have to be focused on just one genre to sell. However, in the beginning keep your pre-order focus similar to the in-stock items you're already selling and branch out from there.

4. **Finding Pre-order Suppliers**

   a. The best way to begin looking for your potential pre-orders is to begin with the suppliers you currently use. Most, if not all suppliers sell pre-orders.

   b. Just locate the section on your supplier's site dedicated to pre-orders. Most sites will have this section separated by months; choose ONE month after the current month, since those are in the future.

   c. Pick a product and copy and paste the title into eBay. eBay may or may not have that product listed. If it does, let's see how much people are charging for it. Based on the charges, if the item is selling for a good price run the numbers based on the formula we discussed for in-stock items.

   d. What is my price for the widget? First, identify what the lowest pre-order item is selling for. Let's say the widget's lowest price is $11.50, so we'll try and sell ours to undercut our competition for $10. Let say again that the widget's wholesale price is $5 per, and let's say you would have to order at least 10 from the website in order to secure your order. Note: This is all for the sake of calculation, you do not order any pre-orders at this point from the supplier's website, you only order pre-order after a certain threshold has been met, we will discuss this more later.

You must factor into this price 12 percent for the shipping fees from the supplier to you. So ($50 x .12) +50 = $56. We must also factor into this price the cost of outgoing boxes and shipping supplies per item. Let's say it will be $1.50 per outgoing item. So $56 +11.50 = $67.50/10 = $6.75/widget

Now we must consider what we plan to sell these units for in eBay. We want to try to sell these $6.75 widgets for at least $10 on eBay. eBay will take around 9 percent commission and PayPal is going to take around 3.5 percent. So let's take $10 x .125 = $1.25. Finally we take $6.75 +$1.25 (eBay + PayPal commission) = $8.00. So $8.00 is the REAL price per item. This means that, if we are able to consistently sell each widget for at least $10, we are making a 20 percent profit, which is fantastic.

So we're basically using the same mathematic approach as we did with in-stock items. This should be done for all items you plan to post for pre-order sales. There are some shortcuts. Again, I recommend creating a spreadsheet in Excel that automatically does this cost estimation for you. You'll also see similar items for sale as a pre-order on your supplier site that you can ballpark all of this math and save yourself time. You'll also get to the point when you can just look at an item and tell if it will sell or not, but that comes with a lot of practice and experience which you will inevitably get as you progress within the system.

5. Pre-Orders are scheduled by month BUT...

Here's a warning about pre-orders, and one reason why they can be tricky. Many times a pre-order will say that it is coming out in February, but then February comes and goes and the item has not shipped. This is the case with roughly half of all pre-orders. Manufacturers will "postpone" many products to gauge customer response, so you need to be prepared for this and have the necessary tools in place when this happens. A few things to help protect you in case this occurs:

Clearly state in HUGE BOLD LETTERS IN YOUR LISTING, as I mentioned earlier, a lot of times when customers come across a pre-order they do not notice that it is a pre-order. They are usually so excited to see an item that they don't pay attention to certain details, or fine print if you will. Since we know that, I like to post this large and clear for the custom write up from along with a small disclaimer underneath. For example:

PRE-ORDER ONLY

INTERNATIONAL SHIPPING AVAILABLE

All pre-orders will be shipped within 30 days of your purchase as per eBay terms and conditions. Acme Store is not responsible for manufacturer delays. We are a retailer and do not control when products are shipped to us from the manufacturer.

(Then I'll continue with the item for sale.)

Superman 12-inch Action Figure

(Description)

In this example, you can see I post it large and noticeable for customers. Even though many won't notice and will still purchase the item and a few will even complain later that you're taking too long to ship; you can always refer them back to the listing they won. Many will feel embarrassed for getting mad at you and will end up keeping their order in with you out of guilt. ;-)

    a.   Another thing to do when your pre-order is delayed is offer refunds profusely. If a customer is angry and demands to know what happened to their item, explain that it was a pre-order and it is running late, refer them to their listing, then let them know if after all of that explanation you'd be happy to give them a refund. Sure, you'll do a few refunds here and there, but most customers are more interested in the item than the money, and will appreciate the fact that you offered to refund them.

    b.   Create a calendar of your pre-order sales. There are plenty of calendar applications available for free. I use Google calendars because it is integrated into Gmail, which is what I use and recommend you using. For every pre-order you sell, mark it on your calendar with that customer's info, create an appointment for 44 days AFTER their item was sold. Why 44 days? Because 45 days is the amount of time the customer has to submit a claim in eBay to receive a refund. More importantly, you are able to refund your customer's money within 45 days and receive a refund on the eBay and PayPal commissions you paid. So it is not a loss to you or the customer. Basically you can sell 10 pre-orders, if it's late you let the customers know about it once that month is over or after your supplier has informed you of the delay (many suppliers won't tell you squat so you either have to ask them or check their website). If you've been keeping your customers up to date with timely responses to their questions and have been proactive with weekly email updates of the item's status, seven out of ten will keep their order in with you until the next month, two will not respond at all to any of your emails, and one may ask for a refund. Either way, after 44 days of each sale if you have not received a shipping confirmation from your supplier, you need to refund all of your customers' orders. Write them a nice straightforward email, letting them know that you do honest business and that this was not your responsibility, and you operate within eBay operating procedure as a stand-up seller, blah blah blah. Make sure to include the link to your newly created listing of the product you're refunding them with an updated projected month for release of the pre-order. Many of these customers will buy from you again because you have been up front with them and communicated well. You've also recouped your eBay and PayPal fees since you refunded their money within 44 days. You may lose one or two customers but that's OK. Repeat this process within 44 days for all products that haven't come out when planned. It's foolproof!

6. **Pricing Pre-order Products**

During your research of pre-order products, I'd say about 40 percent of the time you'll see that nobody is selling that item on eBay. Sometimes you can run into a false no show, be sure to scroll down and click on the alternative search recommendations given by eBay, the product you're looking for may be under a slightly different search term. If it's not there, try removing certain meaningless adjectives from the title and you may find the item under that alternative search. However, for 40 percent of the searches where you've tried everything and still nothing shows, then you are lucky! Even with that pre-order item being sold on other suppliers' websites and retailers' sites easily accessible with a quick

Google search, you can list your item HIGHER than all of these because it's not listed yet on eBay. eBay has the perception that it always has the lowest-priced items even when a lot of time it does not!

Since there's no competition on eBay yet to base your price off of, start with the supplier's site and see what the SRP is, go 20 percent higher than that (YES, 20 percent). This is your chance to make a lot of money before others get in on this pre-order. Price it that way and you'll make sales on eBay right away. Eventually, once others get in the market they'll undercut you drastically and kill the revenue being made on this item, but that's OK. I wouldn't even recommend lowering your price too much to compete with them. Just move to different items, you've made your profit here.

7. Keep Track of Pre-orders Sold

When a customer makes a pre-order purchase from you, keep track of their contact info: email, user ID, etc. on a spreadsheet for later usage. This will come in handy once your pre-orders come into stock and to communicate on delays.

Every week, whether the pre-order is on track or delayed, you need to email you customers letting them know that 1) your order is still on track to be released next month (or this month), or 2) you have just received word that the item has been delayed. If it has been delayed ALWAYS offer a refund (most people will keep their order in). ALWAYS KEEP IN THE DATE OF THEIR ORIGINAL ORDER. We discussed placing their orders on a calendar 44 days after their purchase to give refunds. If the item has not shipped to you from the supplier within 44 days, refund the customer's money, thus protecting yourself against a customer refund later where you cannot be refunded your eBay and PayPal fees.

8. **When to Make Your Orders from the Supplier.**

The beauty of this system is when you make your pre-order sales in eBay, you get your money up front, but when you make your order from your supplier, they don't charge you until the item comes in stock. This is a huge advantage for someone who may not have a credit card or a reserve of cash. While you're waiting on the pre-order to come in, you can use the customer's money to buy supplies, order more in-stock items, or whatever. By the time it comes in, you've moved on to other pre-orders that will eventually pay for the one about to be charged. But when do you order from the supplier?

So, you've sold a few items from a pre-order listing; let's say you've sold three of a particular item in two days. First and foremost, unless you've sold at least three or four units of an item, or unless you are absolutely certain that it will be a huge seller and you are getting a great price, don't bother ordering yet. The instinct to know when to buy a pre-order comes with time and it's not recommended until you've been selling in-stock for a few months successfully. Going back to the example, if you've sold three items you have to be careful how many MINIMUM quantities you are required to order by your supplier. Some SKUs may require you to purchase 12, some may only require you to buy two. If the three items you've sold are selling for $80 each, and the supplier requires you to buy 12 at a time, then you will want to make your order. Remember, your competition WILL come eventually and you want to have already sold a ton of units with only a few left, you do not want to over order. Suppliers do not refund kindly on orders, they make their orders from the manufacturer, and manufacturers do not allow refunds.

What I suggest instead is not to even list an item that requires you to purchase a larger amount than you think you can move and make a profit on. If the price of the item is $8 each, and the supplier requires you to purchase a large amount, then the risk is not as high as it is when the price per item is higher. I purchase high-price items, don't get me wrong, and I think you should too, just make sure it is something with a lower item-count requirement to purchase.

Once you've sold 70 percent of the minimum purchase from the supplier I'd say you could go ahead and make your order from them. If the minimum is six items and you've sold two, wait. If you've sold four, go ahead and only order the six, no more! Consider again that delays will happen and you never know when. If you've sold four out of six and there's a delay, then you may lose one or two of your sales before the item is released. Once it's released, the competition will be ridiculous and margins will be slim, you will have to get your profit from the buyers who kept their order in and sell the rest at cost to prevent a loss.

9. **Once the Pre-order Item Comes into Stock**

You should receive a notification from your supplier when your pre-order comes into stock. If they don't notify you, you will at least see a charge on your credit card; from there you can check with your supplier to see which pre-order is being shipped. As soon as you receive notice from your supplier that your item is shipping, refer back to your pre-order spreadsheet and email all of your customers that have orders in that their items are being shipped to you from your supplier.

Usually your supplier will ship out in two or three days, and depending on how far you are from your supplier you may not actually receive your stock for at least a week after you are first notified and charged for your pre-order purchase. Do not make any delivery timetable promises to your customer. Just say, "As soon as our stock is delivered to us we will ship your item to you same day. Thank you for your patience."

It is very important to let the customers know that their item is on its way to you, because remember, you are not the only seller of this item. And if you have been able to sell your pre-order at a higher SRP than your competitors because you posted the item first, the likely outcome is for your customers to eventually notice and request a refund. You don't want this, because they may be upset to see this item selling for much less than they bought it for. The email you send once you're notified puts out the fire before it happens, they are not as inclined to check online for their product elsewhere, thus never seeing other prices, thus keeping their order with you and you making a huge profit per item!

10. Adhere to eBay Policy

There will be times while you're selling that you think you are untouchable, sometimes you'll make more money in a day than you ever have in a month. Sales will be coming in left and right and you may become sloppy. Be sure to ALWAYS respect the power of eBay and always know, especially when you're doing great, that they are watching you and will shut you down if you don't respect their policies. A few things to always keep in mind:

a.   Strive for great feedback; a few bad feedbacks will kill your business. Literally, nobody will buy from you again, unless your feedback is in the thousands you might as well start over. Keep in mind eBay has a feedback forgiveness system in place, you are able to communicate with the customer who left you the bad feedback and work with them to get it reversed or at least a neutral, there are only five "feedback forgiveness's" per year so don't rely on this!

b.   Don't try to sell pre-orders that are more than a month out. If it's February don't try to sell any pre-orders after March. The eBay compliance team will shut your store down or suspend those listings.

c.   Refund customers right away. Sometimes you may get busy or say to yourself, "I'll get to that tomorrow." Don't fall into that trap, refund customers right away and they'll be more likely to buy from you in the future, and you will avoid them opening complaints in PayPal in which that money gets frozen anyway. You'll also likely receive bad feedback if you don't refund their money promptly.

d.   Don't forget to refund orders that are more than 44 days old right away, or you won't be reimbursed by eBay or PayPal.

11. Capital is King

As with any business, capital and cash flow are key. One thing that's great about *The Profit Principle* system is that it teaches you to use the customer's money in order to operate your business. Even with the customers' money, you'll still need SOME money to begin. I started my first internet venture with $400, and that paid for my LLC paperwork, inventory, and a copy of QuickBooks. If you don't have things like a computer or printer, then you may need more. If you are able to get a business credit card, I recommend using that only for all purchases, it will become vital once you become larger and your pre-orders start rolling in. You can benefit from the massive amount of inventory you'll order along with other expenses and most credit cards have reward plans, I rack up two or three free round-trip tickets a month using my points, and eventually you will too.

5
AMAZON

Selling on Amazon is a little different than eBay. First of all, Amazon does not allow pre-orders unless you're a mega retailer. I use Amazon as an additional avenue to sell my in-stock items. I greatly prefer eBay, not only because it allows pre-orders, but because items typically sell for a lot higher on eBay than Amazon. Amazon also requires there to be existing listings available of the products you're trying to sell, so if you have more obscure products you won't be able to sell on Amazon. However, I do want you to create a selling account on Amazon because you can list all of your in-stock items and they will move, slowly but consistently on Amazon. Amazon does not have auction-style listings like eBay, they are all fixed price. Amazon also does not integrate with PayPal, it sends the money directly to your bank account via credit card or account information. When you set up your account, be sure to use your company credit card or banking information. Listing items on Amazon is a lot faster, you simply perform a search for the product you're looking to sell, find the lowest priced item and to the right you'll see a link that says, "sell yours here." Follow that link and add the price you're willing to sell it for.

One note: even though the prices on Amazon may be a lot lower than you want to sell your item for, don't haggle with customers. You have a successful business on eBay already, so post the price you want to sell the item for, not what everyone else is selling for. You are not able to enter a shipping price as well. Amazon takes the weight of the item based on its ASIN number and judges what the average shipping costs may be and that is the amount credited to your account once the item sells. You will find Amazon a nice accompanying piece to your business, especially when you've overreached on ordering products and you need to move them fast!

6

FULFILLMENT CENTERS

1. Why Not Use Them from the Beginning?

A fulfillment center is a company specializing in product fulfillment services, on behalf of the product owner. In other words, they receive, house, package, and ship YOUR inventory for you. You can send inventory directly to them that you have in stock, or you can arrange for your products to ship from your supplier directly there. So why am I just now mentioning fulfillment centers? Why have I not come out from the beginning telling you to send your entire inventory directly there?

Some books will tell you to automate from the beginning. Well, that may be correct in some cases; it is not the correct approach when creating an online retail business. The reason? MONEY! When you begin selling online you will make a lot of mistakes, there's no way around it. Hopefully you will not make many of the mistakes I have since you're reading *The Profit Principle*, but there will be things outside the confines of this system that you will inevitably do wrong.

And when you make mistakes in business, they usually mean losing money. Once you have relatively mastered the ART of selling on eBay and the complexities of the pre-order process, you are ready for a fulfillment center. This is for karate green belts, not white. When you've shipped products yourself and mastered the pricing schemes associated with different shipping services and companies, you'll understand weights of products and how each weight and service are shipped internationally and domestically.

So you may still say, "Screw shipping myself, I don't want to learn any of that, let the fulfillment center handle that for me." Well, going back to my reason for holding up on the fulfillment centers—money. Fulfillment center are not free: news flash, right? They charge you a storage fee based on the dimension of each of your items and that is typically a monthly fee. They also charge a handling and packaging fee when they ship out your items. Once you have been working the system yourself for a few months by yourself, you will have a better idea what your profit margins are on each item and you will be able to afford a fulfillment center.

Now that we've gotten all of the doom and gloom out of the way, the bottom line is that ultimately you MUST move to a fulfillment center or else your house will be overrun with products, and trust me, it happens fast. The above piece is really just a disclaimer as to why I think you should wait until you have worked your business yourself. I want you to remain profitable as you use the fulfillment center. Using them too soon may lead to you breaking even or losing money, which is not what we're about right?

2. Fulfillment by Amazon

Fulfillment centers were once regional and only set up for the big boys to use. Now they are available for any retailer to use. The most popular is Amazon with their 'Fulfillment by Amazon' service or FBA. The biggest plus to using fulfillment by Amazon is that once you ship your items to them for storage, they are also sold on Amazon Marketplace. It is very easy to set up an FBA account, their website is www.amazonservices.com. Once you've signed up, you simply need to search each product you're selling and select the "Sell yours here" button on the right. Once this is done, you'll create a listing for your item and when given the prompt on where the item will ship from, you will select FBA. Amazon gives you a choice of whether you want to ship the item yourself or if you want them to ship it for you. Once you've indicated this, you will begin to set up your shipment, you give it a name and you can add other products to this shipment the same way.

Note: Don't try to load all of your items into a box prior to listing them on Amazon. Some items, usually based on size, will be shipped off to different Amazon fulfillment centers. As you list them, you will receive the option to add them to existing shipments, in which case you can add those items to an existing box. Or you will receive the option to create a new shipment. If it doesn't show the other shipments you've named, then you know that you'll need to ship separate boxes as this will be going to a different location. Once your box or boxes are full, you enter dimensions, weight, and quantity of each SKU and you're ready to ship. I recommend using your UPS account to ship these and Amazon will give you that option.

Once you've shipped your entire stock of products, you are now able to automate this process for the future. As you receive notifications of your pre-orders coming into stock, go ahead and create a listing on Amazon for those items. You will not be able to create a listing for your pre-orders on

Amazon until Amazon has received notification from the manufacturer that the product is now available.

Once you've been charged for that pre-order by your supplier, it should be by that time searchable on Amazon, since the manufacturer will alert Amazon first when new products are released. Once you've created the listing for the newly in-stock pre-order, you will see to which fulfillment center each product is being shipped; alert your supplier to ship that item to that address in an email. Ask them to give you an estimate of the dimensions or the items' weights so that you can set up the shipment in FBA. For this situation, use your own FedEx or UPS account number to ship, and you'll see options in Amazon where you can let them know that this is how these packages will be shipped. This will allow you to NEVER receive products into your home, which is what you want. It takes you out of the loop and lets you operate your business over web and email. You are getting close to the dream! Once you receive an order on eBay, you simply login to your FBA account, select the item(s) sold and enter your customer's address. The item is shipped that day! No more late nights shipping items and boxes everywhere. Just enter in their address and Amazon handles the rest.

The biggest advantage FBA has on other fulfillment centers is that it sells your products on Amazon while they are in their inventory, and ships them out for you. However, this convenience does not come without its own perils. I have had situations where I may only have one or two of an item and it sells on eBay and Amazon, and now I have to either try to scramble and order the item again (usually at a lost to me since competition is now fierce) or refund my eBay or Amazon customer. You will also run into situations where you forget to take down the item from either eBay or Amazon and the same situation occurs. The best way to handle this is to give eBay priority. If you are selling items with low quantity, do not list that item on Amazon. I give eBay priority because your products usually sell for more there, so we want to make as much money as possible. To do this, take down the listing for the item selling with the small quantity. Amazon will still store this item, they just don't sell it any longer on your behalf, which means you'll have to input the customers address from eBay once it sells.

The biggest negative when dealing with FBA is how it handles international orders. For some reason Amazon will ship your international orders when the customer purchases via Amazon, but they will not ship international orders that come from elsewhere. And international orders are where you will get 40 to 50 percent of all of your business, so that creates an issue!

So how do we handle this? Again issues like this are why fulfillment centers are not at the beginning of this program. What I recommend you do is this: for fast moving items, in eBay do not set them up with international shipping availability. You'll only recognize a fast-moving item based on experience and your metrics. Fast-moving items will sell in enough time for you to make your profit, and you can afford to sell them all within the U.S. Certain items only sell internationally regardless of whether they are fast or slow moving. For slow-moving items, you can keep them listed both on Amazon and eBay to help speed the process of selling them. If you do sell one of these slower items internationally, there are a couple of options. One would be to request Amazon to send that item back to you and you can send it to your customer from there. If you recognize certain items usually ship internationally, you may want to search for other fulfillment centers for those items that do offer the option of shipping internationally.

3. Math on Fulfillment Centers

Most Fulfillment centers will price services similarly. FBA, for instance, charges a storage, weight, handling, and pick and pack fee. They also charge an order-handling fee if the item isn't sold on Amazon. The storage costs may vary from fulfillment center to fulfillment center, but this is basically calculated based on the item's dimension within its packaging. Weight handling is for the effort to move your items around their warehouse. Pick and pack fee is picking the item from its location in the warehouse, packaging the item properly, and labeling it for shipping.

If your item sells on Amazon, you need to be aware of this cost as well as the commission Amazon charges per transaction sold. It's usually between $1.40 and $2.00 for storing and picking and packing, and then their nine percent commission, depending on the price of the item. This could result in lower-priced items not making much of a profit. Should you still use a fulfillment center for lower priced items then? I say yes, a lot of lower-priced items already have a small margin, so many of these I find are only useful to boost my feedback score through successful transactions—feedback that I'll need to get higher-priced pre-orders items sold with a large profit margin!

7

VIRTUAL ASSISTANT

This will be the final step to complete automation of your e-commerce empire. Below you will learn about virtual assistants and how they can run your business for you, that includes answering all customer emails, selecting products to post on eBay and Amazon, even how to price them. All without you so that you can do what you want while your business makes money on your behalf!

4. Intro to Virtual Assistants

A virtual assistant, or VA, is anyone who can remotely access information on your behalf. They can be individuals or companies who hire and assign VA's to clients. Traditionally, the most used VA's are in Asia where the cost for labor is cheapest. The perception in America is that Asian workers will not produce the same level of quality as American workers. This is not true. What I have found is that the VA is really only as good as the person managing him and the instructions given. If you are in constant contact with your VA, you will have no trouble managing them.

5. oDesk

There are many sites available online to find a quality VA, but the one I recommend is oDesk (odesk.com). oDesk is an online platform where you can find anything from artists to software developers. It is made up of freelance individuals looking to make money on the side as well as established companies looking for an additional source of revenue. The first thing you need to do is create your company profile. Link your bank account to this profile for future payments. oDesk is set up so that you or anyone on your team can access the account and manage your VAs. oDesk gives you the option to pay hourly or a fixed price. You can create weekly budgets for your VA, so they do not exceed your budget. oDesk also has a killer feature called Work Diary that is an application on your VA's computer that takes snap shots every few seconds of their screen and saves it for you to view later. It also records their time spent working on your project and you only pay for the time spent. The Work Diary is only available for hourly projects, as you wouldn't need to see the screen and track hours on a fixed-price project.

Once you've set up a profile on the site, you can post your project. In our case, you will be posting a project for a long-term VA with e-commerce and customer service background to run your online shopping sites. Choose the category of the post then write a short description of what you're looking for and skills required. Skills would be: fluent in English, MS Office, experience with e-commerce database creation and site maintenance. Experience with eBay and Amazon a plus. That's usually good enough to get a post out there. You'll also be asked to post a dollar amount for the project. Choose hourly and about $1.00 or $1.50 per hour. Yes, you read that right $1.00 to $1.50 per hour! Around the world, the dollar carries a lot further than it does in the states. You're going to end up hiring someone from Asia at these prices, which is fine, and this amount of money is like paying someone in the US $10 per hour. Besides, most of the VA's aren't just working for you, they'll double dip during the same hours and make double or even triple during the same time span, which is fine for us because we're not paying much anyway!

6. Picking a VA

OK so you've posted your job, you're going to get bombarded with a ton of applicants. The filtering process with the applicants begins by reading their feedback. Each applicant has a profile and that profile will show a feedback and hours worked. If the applicant doesn't have at least a 4.8 to 5.0 and 50 hours worked then don't use them. You don't want to be anybody's guinea pig, you want someone with experience. The second way to filter out applicants is to write the applicants that have the proper ratings reiterating that this contract only pays $1.00 to $1.50 per hour and there is no set numbers of hours that will be worked per week. Some weeks they may work up to 40 hours and some weeks they may only work 10. Ask them to respond and acknowledge that they understand this, along with what available hours they will be online if they were to receive the contract. The third and most effective way to filter out applicants is to chat with them online. If you haven't already, create yourself a Skype account. Request that the remaining oDesk applicants send you their Skype IDs for an interview. Once you do so, carve out a couple of hours to interview them all. Explain what you would like to do.

Job Responsibilities for the VA

a. Search for products to sell using existing pattern of items you're selling. They will use *The Profit Principle* formula determine what to sell.

b. They will list that product on your eBay store site. You will show them how you list them and what you've learned (hopefully from this program). They will list pre-orders and in-stock items.

c. They will make orders from your suppliers for pre-orders sold. Your account information is already available on your supplier's site, so your VA will never actually see your credit card or bank account info.

d. The VA will be responsible for inputting the customer's address into Amazon once sold on eBay.

e. They will be responsible for communication with your customer via email. You can give them access to your email account and they will eventually be responsible for all customer inquiries as well as communication to the supplier.

f. Anything else you throw at them.

As you explain these things to your VA, try and get a feel for their language skills. Ask them frequently if they have questions. See if they have a sense of humor.

Note: Too many smiley faces from your VA conversation means that they didn't fully understand what you just said or they don't know how to respond to your statement in English. Also, if your VA takes a long time to write you back, most likely they are copying and pasting your text into 'Google translate' and copying and pasting the result back to you. Don't get me wrong, Google translate is great. I've used Google translate to communicate to customers in order countries while pursuing a sale. However you don't want to hire someone who is exclusively using a translation tool to communicate. Some words or phrases just don't translate and will be misleading trying to use Google Translate to find out the meaning. You eventually want to be completely out of the loop and only speaking with your virtual assistant, so a more than average grasp of the English language is imperative. Communication is the key to success on the battlefield so getting someone you're comfortable with is crucial.

7. **Training**

Once you have selected your VA, you need to award them the contract via oDesk and now it's time to begin training them to run your ship. At this point you should know roughly what your profits are a week. We will set aside $30 per week for three weeks to get our guy up to speed. The first step in training is setting up a WebEx account or Goto meeting. Webex and Goto meeting are similar services that allow you to share your desktop with someone over the web. You won't need long-term contracts with these sites; you should only need them for one month, two max. Once you have these accounts in place set up a quick outline of topics you want to cover with your VA and begin your meetings. You can either use Skype to call your VA or use the chat system. For this, I've found calling to be a lot easier and Skype has a free VoIP service that allows this. Once you've connected with your VA, introduce yourself and give him an overview again of what is expected. Begin with your eBay store, show him your products. Then show him your suppliers. Show him how you choose which products to list. Ask him frequently if he has questions since he will be doing this himself soon. Show him some emails you've received from customers and let him get a feel for how you like your emails answered. CC him all of your emails going forward. Show him FBA and explain how to input addresses there for sales made on eBay. You are going to spend the next few weeks showing your VA everything you've learned to this point and they you should have the same WebEx session, except you let him perform these functions instead of you. Through WebEx, you are able to give attendees control of the screen and once he has it you can ask him to proceed to show you what he's learned.

8. Starting you Business with a VA

Even though the virtual assistant section is near the end of this system, it does not mean you ABSOLUTLEY have to wait in order to get them involved. If you have disposable income from the beginning, consider hiring the VA from the very start. It will cost you $30 to $40 a week, but you will begin to make money very fast so you will still be profitable. If you are ambitious enough to begin with the VA in tow, they will learn and do as you do. You can follow this system as a guideline and avoid making costly mistakes. Your VA may be ready to go in a few weeks and you will not need any time to train.

9. Waiting for a VA

As you experiment with your product line, money in the beginning may be an issue. Once you've found your niche within a niche, the cost of the VA will be an afterthought, but until you reach that phase, you may want to operate the system yourself with a mind to eventually get the VA involved after a few months. Whatever you do, do not go for more than three or four months on your own. Get the VA involved to run the business and you can monitor their progress and answer any of their questions to you. Remember the goal of this system is for complete automation of your income. The longer you wait the longer it will take to train your VA and the harder it will be for you to let go control of the reins.

10. VA Running the Business

This is self explanatory but worth mentioning again. With the exception of your accounting information, you want the VA to know and be comfortable doing everything in your business. The only thing to closely monitor in the beginning is what they are ordering, but through your trainings you can carefully show them the process of selection so that there can be no mistake or guessing. Also you must always be available to your VA to contact. Many times the VA is just as nervous as you to be running someone else's company and will need additional clarity from you, especially in the first month or so. Make yourself available, eventually their reliance on you will fade and you won't hear from them but maybe once a week with your status update.

8

THE WEBSITE, YOUR STOREFRONT

1. Why Start my Own Website?

Once you make it to this point, you should be a pro in e-commerce. You've been extremely successful on eBay and Amazon; you've completely automated your business with fulfillment center shipping and your VA to handle the day-to-day operations. You may not be considering starting your own website. I will start by saying that this is a great idea and it is recommended EVENTUALLY in this system. I say eventually because there are a few factors that go into a successful e-commerce site. This is a different beast than eBay or Amazon and should be handed as such.

Cost of ownership is much higher. You need to know up front that to build a successful and attractive ecommerce site it will cost you between $500 and $2,000 to do properly. If you've been selling on eBay and Amazon exclusively for at least six months and using this system, you should be making between $8,000 and $15,000 a month depending on what type of items you're selling. With some of that cash, you can build you a very professional-looking website, and don't be cheap. Cheap in, cheap out. You can get anyone to build a website, but if it looks like crap, guess what, you won't make one sale, guaranteed. You have to keep in mind that you are unheard of at this point. eBay and Amazon spend millions just in advertising their brand and when you sell on one of those sites you're able to benefit from their branding. However, a website gives you an additional way to sell in stock items as well as another way to sell pre-orders. An e-commerce merchant will charge a lot less commission than eBay and Amazon, so this is always a way for you to save money.

2. Yahoo Store or Another Cart?

Once you decide to build your website, you have to decide which e-commerce solution is right for you. There are a lot of players and most are very similar, but the one I recommend you use is Yahoo Stores. Yahoo Stores is used by many of the largest e-commerce sites out there. The setup is easy and it has a lot of marketing options within the admin tool, which make it very useful for promotions and affiliates. It's also a trusted name and someone you don't have to worry about their servers crashing and you not being able to sell your products because of outages.

3. Elance or oDesk to Design my Site

Yahoo Stores comes with a few garbage free templates, avoid these like the plague. As I mentioned before, you will need to hire a professional website developer to design your site. Come up with a catchy name that describes your business, then register that domain on godaddy.com or domain.com. Look for Yahoo Store developers online and on Elance and oDesk. Be sure that developer has a portfolio for you to look at, and they specialize in the Yahoo's proprietary language of RTML. You may find a great website developer, but if they don't know RTML they cannot design

Yahoo Stores sites. The site should cost between $500 to $2,000 to build, and will likely take around three weeks to get right. Once you have a site you like, pay the developer and begin to load your products.

4. Google Analytics

Make sure your developer adds Google Analytics to your website; it will help you to identify which search terms are bringing traffic to your site as well as the total number of hits you get for a date range. It is also great in conjunction with AdWords to see how your marketing campaigns are progressing. This is a must for any webmaster, get it, it's free!

5. Loading products

This is something I suggest you do only once and only just so you know how to explain it to your VA. This is a very time-consuming process so the VA is perfect for this. Yahoo stores do allow you to submit a CSV batch file to quickly load your products, but somebody has to create that. You'll need to list all of the products you have available on your eBay and Amazon sites, including all in-stock and pre-order items. The pricing to list these is a little trickier than it is on eBay. Since most of your business will come from Google searches, it is important to know what price your items are being sold for online. Run a search on each of the items you plan to sell online just to get an idea. For in-stock items and pre-orders already sold: if you find that the competition is drastically cheaper than your site, then let them scrabble for the crumbs. It's not worth going broke trying to compete with them. If you only have one or two items left from an in-stock or existing pre-order then you may want to consider dropping the price just to move on from the product, but if you still have a lot and have not made the profit, then you want to keep your price the same. Those other websites will eventually run out and people will be banging on your door for that item. If the competition's prices are little less than yours, lower yours slightly, always keeping in mind your profit. If they are higher than your product, then either leave yours the same or raise it slightly. Yahoo Stores charge $39.99 a month residually, so you should be able to pay for that within the first few hours of your first day.

6. From eBay to My Website?

Yup, that's right. eBay charges you close to a 9 percent commission on each sale. Amazon charges close to 10 percent. Yahoo Store charge 1.5 percent, and considering you can integrate your PayPal account with your Yahoo store this is a no-brainer. You will eventually want to start migrating your customer base over to your Yahoo store so that you can make more profit per item sold. The best way to do this is to edit your eBay and Amazon thank-you letter, letting them know that your same items are also sold on your website and usually at a discount. Eventually people will begin to purchase from your website instead of eBay, especially repeat customers. Another way to steer traffic over is to change the signature on your emails and include your company URL. Curious people will click and see that the prices are slightly lower and will purchase from your site. Your feedback in eBay and Amazon are key for your website's success as well, because they are all the customer has to go on when deciding to buy from you outside of eBay or not. Also, as your store becomes more and more popular your products will show up in search results along with your eBay products and the feedback of your eBay store. If someone thinks you have poor feedback on eBay they will not buy from your website period.

7. **BBB, Truste.com, PayPal verified.**

Register with these services to help bring credibility to your website. They are free to sign up for. They won't approve you right away but will eventually and will drive more business to your site.

8. **Domains.com**

Most people have heard of services like godaddy.com and there are several other options out there to register your URL. Since you will be using Yahoo Stores for hosting, you won't have to worry about paying for that portion of their offering. I recommend you use Domains.com to register your domain. They allow you to keep your name private as the domain owner in case someone runs a "whois" search on you. I don't know about you, but I enjoy my privacy. Once you receive your domain, you can give your developer the credentials and they will link the Yahoo store they're building for you to that domain name.

9

ADVERTISING

Advertising your website can be a very tempting action and is useful at times. It can also become a very expensive method to bring traffic to your site—one that could do more harm financially than help if you are careful.

1. Google AdWords

When you first launch your website I feel it is a good idea to advertise aggressively in order to get the word out about your site, and the best place to begin to receive mass attention is Google AdWords. AdWords is a PPC (Pay-Per-Click) advertising service by Google. If you've ever run a search on Google and noticed the ads at the top and to the right, well those are PPC Ads brought to you by AdWords. The way it works is you set up an AdWords account on Google (https://adwords.google.com). You begin what they call a campaign; the campaign allows you to select keywords to begin. For example, if you're selling sports memorabilia the keywords you may use would be "sport memorabilia," "baseball cards," "autographed," etc. Then you select an amount or CPC (cost per click) you're willing to pay for every person that clicks your ad, the more you spend the higher your ad will show up in a search. Finally, you create a daily budget, once you've reached your limit, your ads will stop displaying when searched. I recommend advertising your site for the first two weeks using a very small daily budget, maybe $5 a day in the beginning until you get the hang of what is working, then maybe $10 a day. You'll be able to see which users came to your site through the AdWords portal and also Google Analytics which you should now have on your site. You can create multiple campaigns to target different geographical locations as well as different keywords. These campaigns can be rotated automatically by choosing that setting in AdWords. After two weeks though, if you have not seen an ROI by using AdWords, quit.

2. Word of Mouth

The best advertising you can ask for is word of mouth. Keep the customers you have happy and they will always return to you and send your items around the web to friends.

3. Keep your site updated

Most of your free traffic will come from Google searches, and keeping your site visible will come primarily by keeping your site up to date. In-stock items, top-selling items, new pre-orders, just released items, items that are out of stock, backordered items. All of these need to be kept up to date. I suggest checking pre-orders weekly, and your in-stock and back ordered items daily. You can instruct your VA to perform these duties on your behalf. You'll see that when your site is up to date, 60 percent of your traffic will be due to Google searches that these products will show up under.

4. **Twitter and Facebook**

Once you've built your website it's time to set up a Twitter and Facebook account for your company. On your "Contact Us" link on your webpage include the links to these pages and you'll see your following grow. You can send out product info, new releases, and news. I especially like Twitter because of the "retweet" capability, you can tweet product news and your following has the ability to retweet your tweet to their followers. Birds of a feather flock together, so most likely your followers will have friends with similar interested who follow them, thus increasing your message exponentially for FREE!

5. **Promotional codes**

Yahoo Stores has a great feature that allows you to create promotional codes for your product, categories, or the entire site. These are great if you want to run a sale, create a coupon code of "FREESHIP", tweet it out to your followers and watch as the traffic pours in. It is also great to see which medium works best. Create a different coupon code for Google, Facebook, and Twitter, all offering five percent off and see which one brings in more business. After awhile you can just focus on the medium that proves the most useful.

6. **Affiliates**

Yahoo Stores also has the ability for you to create affiliate links. Affiliates advertise your products on their website for a commission. The way it works is, say you're running a Specialized Coin website and you want to partner with a Coin Blogger. You create the blogger an affiliate link that he can use on his site, the blogger may use your logo or an image you provide him as the graphic as a banner to your site. Once a person clicks on that banner, it will send them to your site and any product they purchase you and your affiliate will be able to track, whatever compensation you have set the affiliate link up with will also show up so that you are both able to see what is owed. At the end of the week, or month, pay out all commissions. This is a great way to drive traffic to your site without spending advertising bucks and it's a "win win" for all involved.

7. Constant Contact

Email Marketing is another popular method to drive traffic to your site for a low cost. Yahoo Store has the ability for customer or potential customers to sign up for your newsletter. As you accumulate customers, keep them in a spreadsheet and once you get 50 or so consider using a service like Constant Contact to send your promotional emails. The cost ranges from $15 to $30 a month depending on how many users you send to. The advantages of programs like Constant Contact over sending the email through a regular POP account is that you are able to run metrics on your emails sent. Things like number of people who opened the email, geographical reporting, email templates for graphics, customers can sign up or opt out using the email. There are a ton of reasons to use this sort of service, it is very affordable, and you are able to track your ROI to see if it's worth it.

10

CONCLUSION

I have laid out here in *The Profit Principle* a path to freedom; the freedom from your unfulfilling job, the freedom to choose how YOU want to live, and the freedom to be creative. If you follow the steps listed, you will have a thriving business that will make you rich and free to pursue that beach living lifestyle many of us strive to reach one day. So go get started!

.

APPENDIX

- Google: secretary of State (your state)
- freelegalagent.com
- quickbooks.intuit.com
- quicken.intuit.com
- www.godaddy.com
- www.domain.com
- shop.usps.com – free boxes
- www.usps.com
- www.fedex.com
- www.ups.com
- www.dhl.com/
- www.uline.com/
- www.officedepot.com
- http://www.usps.com/receive/businesssolutions/poboxesonline.htm
- https://www.google.com/voice?pli=1#inbox
- Google, "custom Logo design."
- www.experian.com
- www.dnb.com
- www.vistaprint.com
- www.ebay.com
- www.amazon.com
- www.paypal.com
- checkout.google.com/
- www.odesk.com
- www.elance.com
- translate.google.com
- www.google.com/analytics
- www.bbb.org
- www.truste.com
- www.domains.com
- adwords.google.com
- www.clickbank.com
- www.constantcontact.com

www.ingramcontent.com/pod-product-compliance
Lightning Source LLC
Chambersburg PA
CBHW022132170526
45157CB00004B/1850